AROMATICS

ALSO BY
ROBERT B. SHAW

POETRY

Solving for X (2002)

Below the Surface (1999)

The Post Office Murals Restored (1994)

The Wonder of Seeing Double (1988)

Comforting the Wilderness (1977)

CRITICISM

Blank Verse: A Guide to its History and Use (2007)

The Call of God: The Theme of Vocation in the Poetry of Donne and Herbert (1981)

AS EDITOR

Henry Vaughan: Selected Poems (1976)

American Poetry since 1960: Some Critical Perspectives (1973)

Aromatics

Poems

Robert B. Shaw

PINYON PUBLISHING
Montrose, Colorado

Cover Painting: John Singer Sargent, *Fumée d'Ambre Gris*
Photograph of Robert B. Shaw by Susan Moore

First Edition: April 2011

Pinyon Publishing
23847 V66 Trail, Montrose, CO 81403
www.pinyon-publishing.com

Library of Congress Control Number: 2010940937
ISBN: 978-0-9821561-9-3

Acknowledgements

Some of these poems have appeared in the following publications:

Alabama Literary Review: "Memory," "The Children," "Working Out," "In the Picture," "River and Road," "Old Man of the Mountain," "Single File"

American Arts Quarterly (web version): "Donors"

The Evansville Review: "Blue Period Sketch," "Habit"

First Things: "Parable of the Birds," "The Better Part of Valor," "Sundial in the Rain," "'The Devil in the Clock,'" "Mirror Verse"

The Hopkins Review: "Experiment in April"

Ironhorse: "Tantalus"

The Raintown Review: "Thresholds"

Shenandoah: "A Spirit Photograph: W. B. Yeats and Another"

Southwest Review: "Hill Towns in Winter"

The Yale Review: "Wild Turkeys"

"In Storage: A Calder Cat" appeared in *Words for Images: A Gallery of Poems*, ed. John Hollander and Joanna Weber (New Haven: Yale University Art Gallery, 2001).

"A Beginning, a Middle, and an End" was the Phi Beta Kappa poem at Yale University in 2002.

For Rachel Hadas

Bad times give way to worse.
Whatever blight's in style,
we cling to thinking verse
is something worth our while.

In these dejected days,
some lines I linger on
are yours, drawn from the maze
surrounding Helicon.

The zodiac revolves.
But words in firm array
outwear what time dissolves,
say what we live to say.

Contents

WILD TURKEYS

Out of the woods and into the side yard
they come in a slow march, a band of three,
dowdy, diagonal in somber plumes
that so englobe their awkward, ambling bodies
it is hard to believe their pipestem legs
truly support them as they promenade.
Their raw red necks and bare heads—slaty blue—
go with the legs, austere, deliberate, wiry,
seconding every step with a prim nod,
while now and then pausing to stoop and nip
whatever seeds or beetles their bead-eyes
have got a bead on. When they reach the foot
of the hill they advance gamely, helping themselves
with little hops and only a faint stirring
of wings, going up with uncanny lightness,
almost as though inflated (which in a sense
they are, given the air caught up inside
their fusty basketry of quills and pinions).
Whether on forage or reconnaissance,
they know where they are going with no hustle;
they are as much unwavering as wild.
Soon they pace out of sight, three emissaries
of shadow taking time to appraise sunshine
on a warm day two weeks before Thanksgiving,
intent as Pilgrims turning out for a hanging.

SCALES

The pink pagoda
has—you can count them—seven
stories, and a roof
with jaunty upturned corners.
It seems a lonesome lookout,

moored amid odd rocks
and odder, rubbery ferns
(or weeds attempting
to pass for ferns) gigantic
enough to dwarf the structure

that one might expect
would dominate them. But this
is nothing compared
to the disproportion of
the golden horde careening

in upper reaches
of the glassy medium
the whole scene is sunk
in, irrevocably steeped:
to any hermit peering

from below the raked
roof, the circulating swirl
of carp would look like
a school of whales patrolling
the heights, flouting undertow.

It's a small boy, though,
no hermit, who appraises
piratic glimmers
cast by the maneuvering
tunics of gold mail. His gaze

swims through the tank—a
bit of live wallpaper most
patrons don't notice,
absorbed in and absorbing
their pricy dabs of sushi.

THE ODOMETER

It was long ago, in the days before seatbelts.
They were all jammed into their secondhand Chrysler,
      three children rumpusing in back,
their zookeepers up front, off to the store

on a hot summer Saturday, when the driver
noticed that something mildly educational
      was about to occur before
their eyes, if they would all pipe down and pin

said eyes to the dashboard. On it, the mileage glowed
faintly at 99,999. In a minute
      they would see a Hundred Thousand
announce itself. The children held their breath.

And then the dénouement: no more room on the gauge,
so what came gliding up was not the number they
      had fizzing in their minds. Instead:
zero, zero, zero, zero, zero.

After a second of befuddlement, the two
older brothers giggled and yelled, "The car is new!"
      The youngest sat back scornfully.
No matter what they said, he knew it wasn't.

He was right: their traveling ambience altered
not a jot. The worn upholstery's dust-imbued,
        dry-roasted smell, the pennies lost
down cracks with stray gum wrappers—all stayed put.

Up front, gripping the wheel a little tighter, their
father thought, *Another couple thousand, and*
        this heap gets traded. Their mother
felt rather than thought, *Some things go too far*

to think about starting over again, and soon
nobody noticed the no-longer-magical
        numbers running, the children now
muffled by a candybar split three ways.

AROMATICS

I

The candle factory's display room runs
about the length of half a football field.
Under its warehouse trussing and the hard
fluorescence pouring down, the aisles teem
with candle mavens bending over bins.
Hanging from crook'd elbows are the baskets
that might once have cradled new-laid eggs;
here, each one is soon lined with a stash
of pick-your-own-assortment votive charmers.
Color-coded roughly along a spectrum—
at one end white, the other black, and in
between, three milling aisles of wax rainbow—
the nubbins nestle like the tips of crayons
destined for giant children, though the wicks
tufting them plainly indicate their function,
and reconfirm them as a fireman's nightmare.

Candles—in this enlightened age, who needs them?
Everyone and his mother, it appears.
And what they're after more than anything
is opportunity to choose aromas.
Only their free-range sniffing can determine
which of these mood-enhancers match their craving,
and which of them are not worth sniffing at.

For each patron bee-lining it to Balsam
or Bayberry (stick-in-the-mud scents),
ten are smitten with selections named
like plein-air studies by Impressionists:
Nantucket Noon, Spring Showers, Mountain Meadow.
Others make one think of dessert menus:
Spiced Apple, Chocolate Cupcake, Key Lime Pie.
Each item offers its particular
sensation, more or less in keeping with
its label's promise. Harder to describe
is the effect of all these scents combining,
making a nectared atmosphere so dense
that one looks up expecting to see clouds
of some uncannily perfumed miasma.
Five parts myrrh to four parts bubblegum?
But that's not really it: the odor's so
composite, swaddling, and synthesized
it leaves the ordinary nose confounded.
Stepping out into the open air,
one needs a moment to recover what
the rank world habitually smells like:
sun-beaten asphalt, parking-lot exhaust,
a big dog trotting past who needs a bath.

II

Sensory overload can be a more
decorous and exclusive exercise.
Recall the Meiji era's "incense parties"
mistily but evocatively sketched
by Lafcadio Hearn in a choice chapter
(see *In Ghostly Japan*). Envision each
kimonoed esthete bowing toward the censer,
essaying to identify each scent
with an allotted set of inhalations.
Imagine what a pungent satisfaction
it must have been to rightly tell apart
Plum Flower's wraith from that of Evening Dusk
or Dew-on-the-Mountain-Path. At intervals,
to reawaken numbed olfactory nerves,
the guests would rinse their mouths with vinegar.

III

Much of a muchness . . . odorous bombardment,
whether democratized or rarefied,
leaves us at length unable to sort out
what we are smelling, or remember it.
It's the less pressing attars that impress.

In the net-curtained house of childhood,
Grandmother's alabaster jar once sat,
its lid cracked and providently mended,
waiting for your inspection. Carefully
(and furtively, now knowing how the lid
behaved when dropped), you uncovered the trove
of vintage, forty-year-old potpourri.
The hoarded petals long had lost their blush;
they might have been tobacco shreds to look at.
But there was still—amazingly—a fragrance
kept for a child's nostrils to ensnare,
the ghost of a ghost of a rose upon the brink
of utter vanishment into the dull
air of the front parlor. You could sense it
smoldering in the heatless fire of time,
each time fainter yet never fully spent—
an emanation now in its way still there
years after your last clandestine tryst,
wisping up when memory lifts the lid.

PLAQUES

Lost in a bronze blur, those dowdy oblongs.
Here, and here, and here is where it happened,
they want to tell us, but we'll never know
just what it was; it isn't safe to crawl
past at a speed congenial to reading.
Let the inscriptions hang, barely discernible
against the building, boulder, pedestal
each is affixed to, pining to be noticed.
"Near this spot" some worthy died or was born,
practiced law or medicine "in this building,"
signed the surrender or set up a gristmill.
Slaves used to be sold here. This is where
the fire began that burned the whole town down.
Look, the hundred-year flood's high water mark.
And here is where the massacre took place. . . .
Pathetic, somehow, this archival urge
to pin events to settings where they hatched,
inviting, in the yawning gulf of time,
a generation's sensible "So what."
History boiled down to boilerplate
pales to verdigris while the planet whirls.
Everything has to happen somewhere. When
the legends on the weathered metal win
attention, it's by accident, and what
we see in them reminds us of the signs
panhandlers wave to advertise their plights:

"Blind"—"Disabled"—"Veteran Out of Work"—
all the disasters, blunders, and outrages
that fell wide of us, so far savaging others,
and that with all our restless hearts we wish
we had the power to forget more fully.

MIRROR VERSE

Brightly it gapes at the room. Nothing can argue the glass
out of its passive (but wait: impassive, call it) alert,
ready and able to mate doubles in pitiless pairs,
mimicking background as well, fixed in its quicksilver depth.
Threatened by such unappeased ardor to match what appears
with a relentlessly true witness to each crooked seam,
blemish or wrinkle or stain? Switch off the light and reflect:
all that the mirror can show cannot correctly portray
which is your right or your left. Nor can it see much beyond
frame-edge, or back of your eyes. Here, as the Book says, we see
through a glass darkly and no image reveals what it veils.
So it may be, but the peace drawn from such dicta is faint.
Catching your twin by surprise, there in his face is a sad
look that is equally yours, longing for something unseen.

TANTALUS

The water, pure as any in a dream,
lapping his legs, the plump and purple fruit
tugging the bough down close enough for him
to smell the ripeness—these were practiced props.
They carried out their orders to the letter,
fleeing his reach of hunger or of thirst
as quickly as his muscles tensed and twitched,
as absolutely as his need struck home.
After the first couple of thousand years
it was predictable. Something less predictable
happened over the next few thousand to
his attitude (and this was very strange,
for isn't life eternal said to be
immutable?). So subtly it occurred,
he scarcely gauged the change but only knew
one day he didn't want them any more,
wouldn't have sunk his teeth into that plum
or guzzled down that teasing rivulet
for anything that anyone could pay him.
But he could never bring himself to act
accordingly, to own up to indifference.
Odd that desire's end should foster shame.
It was still punishment, but of an altered
character, to watch the dodgy, now-
no-longer-tantalizing imps of appetite
playing their part as he in turn played his,

leaning to grab at that recycled fare
whose grip on his awareness still persisted
centuries after the last pang truly gnawed.
How else now could he live up to his name?

REFLECTIONS OF THE HERO

Even for a demigod
it would be demanding,
more like field surgery
than ordinary mayhem.
An ungainly stroke,
a slash down and back,
such as one might use
to kill a creeping snake.
And this to be performed
while staring in the mirror-
coating of the shield
that Hermes tilted for him,
never at the target.

It took some time to aim.
Speaking of snakes, they coiled
about the Gorgon's skull
in calm, unhissing sleep;
and she, out of whose scalp
they grew in limber tresses,
slumbered just as calmly.
The unblemished aegis
shone like a lesser moon
and held in its convexity
her image for the hero
to study unimperiled.

Proving the most lethal
sight on earth will lose
deadliness in reflection,
he felt the moment hover
in which his shielded view
was centered on her face,
so oddly ordinary,
neither young nor old,
not haggard, not alluring,
just that of any woman
he might meet at the market.
Except for the unnerving
reptilian coiffure,
she might have been his mother
lying down for a nap.

He tried his weapon's weight,
exchanged a nod with Hermes.
Until his arm swept down,
hacking the night in half,
her eyes never opened.
But when the head lay separate
the lids crept back as though
to let her look in the mirror.
The blood, when it ensued,
was plentiful and strange,

more violet than red. . . .
His own eyes seemed to blur.

Clumsily he lifted
the prize by its limp tendrils,
concealed it in a sack.
And in the spattered shield
he caught sight of his face,
alone, almost as stony
as statues of him soon
to be erected, showing
his exploit to the world
in a form safe to look at.

A NEW LIFE

Everyone knows the story. Just when I thought
I was lost, a kindlier fate intervened,
rooted me to the cool ground, a mockery
to the god burning after me, whose fingers
finally lighted on bark instead of flesh.
In no time, it seemed, I grew to be at peace
with the change, and perhaps that was the reason:
this was nothing like time as I had known it,
only an unhurried, tranquil rotation
to whose unthreatening rhythm all my leaves
responded, flourished, gave way, and were replaced.
What no one seems to know is that this idyll
came to an end with just as little warning
as when it started. I have lately wondered
if what happened was triggered by the eclipse.
It was when the midday birds, bewildered, sang
their go-to-bed song that I began to feel
seized everywhere by alarm as nerves awoke
to rattle again their chains of coded sparks.
My sweet sap turned to salt, to the old flavor
of blood and tears. I looked in the old way then
(that is, through tears) to see my earlier form
emerging vulnerable and pallid from
the sheath of bark disintegrating round it.
Once again I was cornered into trading
one set of limbs for another. My hair fell

dense to my shoulders, too heavy to be stirred
by random winds to which my leaves had whispered.
My single tongue hid in my mouth, a stunned lump
incapable as yet of utterance. Still,
none of this could surpass the punishing shock
of my first steps away from stasis: crossing
the mossy turf was like walking on ground glass.

The world's pain was a thing I had forgotten.
I admit, with time (with one step at a time),
I grew accustomed to the new state of things.
The sun slid out from behind the shadow, but
paid no attention as I set out in search
of what I had done without for years, a roof.
It seems that one can get used to anything,
given enough time and a lack of options.
It may be true that every mode of being
offers advantages. Oh, but this new life
of mine would rest more easily on me if
I could forget those seasons that I spent
standing in one spot under the changing sky,
living without expectancy or effort.

"THE DEVIL IN THE CLOCK"
—Auden

As though to clear its throat
or heave a rasping sigh,
precluding contradiction,
the clock lets out a whirr,
an increment of friction
to note the time is nigh
before a single note
begins to strike the time.
With undermining sound
the husky harbinger
anticipates the chime
at every hour's round.
Jealous upstager, bent
on stealing thunder from
the dial's prime event,
it must bear us a grudge
to let no hour come
without a know-all nudge.
How can it be a boon
if momently too soon
it prods us toward a future
blind to our present needs?
That sound! A ripping suture
to show a wound still bleeds.

THE CHILDREN

The children scream. It is hard to believe,
but you can hear them over the harsh racket
of that old wooden roller coaster sounding
ready to shake itself to splinters, shooting
carloads of children up, around, and down.
Or: From the back row of the movie house,
between gulps of Coke, they more than match
screams of the overpaid, defenseless starlet
coming face to face with the living dead.
Or: As they scoot through the pedestrian
tunnel's bottleneck to the raucous beach,
they let the shrillest lung-powered missiles loose
to ricochet off shadowy, dank walls—
echoes besting the road-roar overhead.
All this provides them practice. Now they scream
to juice up the backyard birthday party.
Sweating and itching in a polyester
clown suit, a highschool boy blows up
balloons for them; his made-up funny face
has the usual look of a lipsticked skull.
A plane drops low, trailing its routine drumroll.
The children, sugar-saturated, scream
until the neighbors slam their windows down.
Bang! More bangs. Balloons become barrage.
The grass is soon covered with moist scraps
of rubbery pink, and even now the children

scream and if you close your eyes you might
forget the roller coaster's safety bar,
the celluloid contrivance of the film,
the happy family's covey of protection
moving unconcerned through the gray tunnel,
the plane aligned calm for a clear runway.
There, in your own darkness behind your eyes,
treble piercing the underpinning bass,
you might hear the mess of noise stripped bare
of reassuring context, hear the screams
as helpless commentary on what Mister
Chalky Face is ready to hand out
with a fixed grin to children of all ages.

THE BETTER PART OF VALOR

A would-be body surfer, eight years old,
he fell in with the ocean's mood of calm,
reviewing each low swell as it unrolled
before him its obsequious salaam.

Crossing the fringe of foam with splashing stride,
he found himself knee-deep, waist-deep, and still
nothing swung by worth joining for a ride.
Level and lazy lay the sea. Until

the chastening wave upreared a glassy face,
its towering onset tugging up his eyes
to see it beetling. He was locked in place,
discovering how doom can paralyze.

Punitive pounding, surging overthrow,
churning immersion, brackish aftermath,
it was embarrassing to undergo.
The water was as placid as a bath

after this one leviathan hit land,
leaving him for a time to drip and look
daggers at where he'd been from safe on sand.
It was the oldest lesson in the book

that sank in as he sniffled, nursed a scrape,
and kept his jarred attention on the matter.
He would become a master of escape:
when offered fight or flight he'd pick the latter.

Having survived the deluge, common sense
would hold him back from an unequal brawl
with such a mass of green malevolence
a billion times his age and twice as tall.

Deciding this revived his dampened spirit
somewhat. But as long as he would live,
he'd rate the way it hid till he came near it
with things too deep to fathom or forgive.

IRIDESCENCE

Coming and going on the pigeon's
violet throat, a flash of aqua
each time it dipped or twisted, much like
colors she saw spawned in soap bubbles
under the sun in the draining sink:
those were sights she hoarded, along with
the oil-spill on the rain-dark asphalt,
a shifting bull's-eye target of gold
and green with a wider band of mauve.
Clearly (and as her mother told her)
she needed more to do with herself.

Summer was long, and not much happened
when you were ten. Between marriages,
her mother had a certain amount
of "social life" to which she was not
a party. When she recalled that time
she never pictured her mother dressed
for work, but wearing what she thought of
as "the rainbow blouse"—it must have been
shot silk or something, the way it veered
from ripples of pink to stormy blue.
It looked terrific on her, and that
might have been reason enough to gel
the memory of it. Something more
attached to this, though: on one of those

boring Sundays when she got up late,
she found her mother in the kitchen
after a night out with Mr. X,
still, surprisingly, with the blouse on,
nursing a cooled-off cup of coffee.
Something was off-key. She looked again.
What at first she'd seen as eye-shadow
was a dramatically contused
right eye, a shiner just as vivid
as the prized oil-slick on the driveway.
It was frightening because it was
not entirely unbeautiful.
"What did that?" she breathed. After a gap
the answer: "I ran into a door."
And the door shut on further questions,
then or ever. She remembered, though,
how, as if tinged by the deepening
of her unsettlement, the beaming
day flickered into something darker.

BUTTERFLY AT THE BEACH

Between the swell of dune and swell of tide
the scene's predictable: the wet and wide
horizon, each new breaker's suicide,

the children building castles and the crowd
sprawling on beach towels, variously endowed,
gulls raiding trash cans, the occasional loud

plane out of nowhere. But amid all this, why,
with nodding blossoms not at all nearby,
has one quixotic saffron butterfly

come to survey the doings of the ocean?
Mesmerized by the scent of tanning lotion?
Or subject to some freak wind's random motion,

heaving it on a sojourn over sand?
Without even a beach rose close at hand,
chances of its alighting aren't so grand

unless someone's Hawaiian floral print
(though offering nothing tastier than lint)
should tempt it to inspect each raucous tint.

No caftan or bikini features quite
enough bouquet to snag its appetite.
It courses down the coastline—exit right. . . .

A sense that we ourselves have overstayed
drifts in. All the attention that we paid
to that unflagging aerial parade

yields to a sudden feeling that the place is
more of a desert now, less an oasis.
Fluttering fool wings brightly in our faces,

the bug betrayed no doubt where it should go.
Perhaps beyond these miles of ebb and flow
there may be flowers to feed on. Be it so.

EXPERIMENT IN APRIL

Fireplace ashes, so they say,
will make a balking peony blossom.
Something about potassium.
Putting it to the test, today
I trowel our grate's residuum
around the plant that's playing possum.

I snip a withered stem or two
that spent last year in leafy shirking.
Maybe the pale gray scatter-rug
I sprinkle on the spot will do
as advertised, and finally tug
the striking petals into working.

One russet up-from-under spike,
the tip of this year's iteration,
pierces the cinders that I spread,
vibrant, yet votive-candle-like.
Sending mixed signals: no, not dead,
but loath to live for admiration.

Poking up poker-faced through ash,
its aim is not my satisfaction—
only to bring itself to light.
Separate agendas. Must they clash?
My threadbare hopes have buds in sight,
banking on chemical reaction.

WHAT SHE FOUND

All her life long
(and it was long)
she had a knack
for finding these:
out in the midst
of an uncut lawn,
whenever she wanted,
seemingly,
she could reach down
and deftly harvest
a four-leaf clover,
a summer trophy.
Most of her other
accomplishments
were unremarkable:
knowing the names
of birds and flowers,
making a passable
jelly or piecrust.
Maiden-aunt hobbies
made up her life.

But her reconnaissance
skills outdid us.
Nobody else
had such an eye:

cunningly camouflaged
green on green,
the lucky tokens
were safe from us.
Near to ninety,
she still would find them.

We never knew
what she did with them
until, years after
her unabrupt
but mild departure,
a cache turned up
in a garden book:
pressed between tidy
squares of wax paper,
a good half-dozen
looked up at us,
a squad of little
playing-card clubs
(but four-lobed, freakish),
their stems gone brittle,
their color changed
to the olive drab
of some old knapsack.
Veterans, back
on hand to recall

the luck that missed us
but lit upon her,
untransferable,
such as it was.

OAK LEAVES IN WINTER

The leaves that are the last to leave,
clinging to low-down limbs of oak,
would be, I think, the last to grieve
for greener days gone up in smoke.

Not much to look at, crackly, brown,
dowdy with Gothic points and curves,
durable, like the wood they crown,
they hug resilience in reserves

their more flamboyant counterparts
at the first cold let fly entire.
When the red maples hurled their darts
it was their pride to hold their fire.

Now, having shunned the fusillade
that brought their gaudier neighbors low,
they taunt the season as they fade,
defy the wind, look down on snow.

MEMORY

A book that has contrived to hide itself
from you for months turns up one afternoon
point-blank, as you reach for a nearby volume—
misshelved, of course, and who's to blame for that?
You bring it down and plant it on the table
under a decent light and open it
to where you think you'll find the passage you
were hoping for, ensconced in some eventful
middle chapter. But the spine is tight,
spring-loaded, you might think, so avidly
the pages rise whenever you lift your thumb
and flip back to the outset of the story,
determined that you not skip the beginning
without which, after all, nothing makes sense.

How commonplace it grows to lose your place
when every search withers to retrospection.
There by the window glazed against a view
you know by heart and rarely choose to look at,
the fanned pages practice recalcitrance,
harking back as if they were enraptured
atavists, or as if they gave themselves
up to a breeze you can't feel on your skin.

HABIT

His hand went fishing in the silver drawer,
doing its thing with no express command,
the same as it had done the days before.
What did it know, this practiced helping hand,

ferreting after spoons and forks and knives,
gathering up its clutch of two of each?
Plant habit in the muscles and it thrives;
in absentmindedness it fills the breach.

Disquiet halted him as he was turning
to set two places. What could be the matter?
No. . . . Yes. As if he'd handled something burning,
he let the flatware drop with a dull clatter,

reminded that, from now on, one place setting
would do. His hand would have to learn forgetting.

WAKE

As I have before on such occasions,
I think of other ways to hear the word,
alternatives to plush and polished wood
and your festooned inertia. How about
taking it as imperative, a reveille:
Snap out of it! Get up and smell the flowers!
But that would hardly do, with so much riding
on your tacit agreement to remain
unstirred by ceremony and unstirred
by the embarrassment of those who don't
know what to say or do, withdrawn to corners.

No, what I want to gather now from *wake*
is what the forward surge of the power boat
releases backward: first a jaunty spume
like a white peacock tail, then widening out—
long crests and troughs that make their darker way
across the tremulous nets of lesser ripples
to slap against the pilings of the pier
we cluster on, still boggling at your passing.

THE POE TOASTER PREPARES
FOR HIS ANNUAL VISIT

The weatherman's predicting sleet tonight.
As if I needed one more disincentive . . .
It was Father who was the fanatic.
His self-appointed dive into the Poe
Centennial in 1949
was such a thrill he had to re-enact it,
and did, for more than forty years. If I
should last as long I'll be amazed and grateful.
(Grateful to be alive, I mean, not grateful
to be persisting in this homemade homage.)
Father adored it all: the black fedora,
the scarf masking his face, the silver-tipped
cane he didn't need at first, then did
in his last decade. Faithful to his whim,
he'd slink out every January 19th
in the small hours, the raw Baltimore night,
and make his shadowy pilgrimage to Poe's
belated monument with its carved raven
that doesn't look much different from a seagull.
Ceremoniously he placed oblations:
cognac, a good label, the bottle partly
drained by the ritual drams he'd savored
before venturing out, and three red roses.
("Blood-red" was what the papers always said.)
Steering clear of the poor, sleep-deprived
reporters on the prowl to get a story

as spooky as they could from his routine,
he made his way back home to us, replete
with duty done, the Master's birthday marked.
Finally when it got to be too much
for him, he added to his offerings
a note, unsigned, announcing to the world:
"The torch will be passed." So, from then on, this
became my annual responsibility.

I'd like to say I felt enthusiasm,
but it was something more like resignation.
A Presbyterian churchyard's not the most
cozy of spots in dead of night in winter;
and still, when I see "Toaster" in a headline,
"kitchen appliance" pops up in my head.
Poe, I suspect, could care less. People say
he may not even be beneath that stone,
the wrong set of bones having been moved there.
(Bodies that don't stay put: a theme of his.)
I don't care much for cognac, and in fact,
to get down to it, I can take or leave
that feverish stuff he wrote: the soggy verses,
the tales with nut-case narrators expounding,
the razor-brandishing orang-outang,
the pit—the pendulum—the walled-up cat—
and all those dashes darting round the page.

But there are always readers who succumb
to lines like "Death looks gigantically down."
(That's one that even I think not too bad.)

In any case, I'll see it through tonight.
Father's been gone some years and still it seems
I haven't got the heart to disappoint him.
Nowadays the only hint of challenge
comes in evading what's become a pack
of partyers who crowd the gates to spy
and shiver in the slush. It isn't hard, though.
They won't accost me, having no great wish
to put a mundane end to this enigma.
To them I'm something here in Baltimore
like Pennsylvania's groundhog, showing up
to do my bit dependably in public,
worth a few column inches every winter.
It adds a modicum of atmosphere,
and atmosphere was everything to Poe.
Does he look down gigantically at us?
Poe didn't live for long in Baltimore,
but he's been dead here for a long, long time.

A SPIRIT PHOTOGRAPH:
W.B. YEATS AND ANOTHER

The specter, just as you'd expect, is pale—
the disembodied hovering face appears
almost as chalky (and almost as round)
as a digestive tablet, moored in air
at a sharp tilt, occluding with its haze
the right-hand swag of the poet's regal mane.
Like an invisibly tethered, murkily
lit balloon but for some key details:
lips wistfully parted, a long streak
stained dark as a silent movie star's,
and up above, nose blurred to nothing, eyes
unfocused, or (in this mercurial image)
so *out*-of-focus no intent or sentiment
declares itself in them: a pair of raisins
studding a pallid bun. Below, the poet
patiently sits, affording a distinguished
anchorage for this ethereal waif.

Behind tortoiseshell spectacles, his own
eyes are harbored so deep in their sockets
you cannot see if they are shut or staring,
aiming at inward or at outward vision.
Then too, he might be simply wincing at
a flashbulb's brilliant spasm capturing
the dead communing with the quick in this
improbable tableau. Your first response

might be to giggle (mine was) at this oracle
sedate in tweeds, providing this phantasm
a perch as it takes form out of the dark
(or one might rather say out of the darkroom).

A histrionic apothegm of his
flickers in memory—something to the effect
that there are only two things of interest
to an intelligent person: sex and the dead.
Can it be so? This wan, off-center succubus
doesn't excite much interest either way,
nor is this encounter much of a tryst
since the pair, both facing us straight on,
might even be oblivious of each other.
But they're on the same wavelength, or the same
astral current—so the bland exposure
purports to testify. Designed to prove
the living and the dead share tenancy
here on the dusty earth, preposterous
but unabashed, for all its fakery
the photo makes a viewer muse. The poet's
ache to gaze clear of the cage of bone
is palpable in this as in his art—
how ready are we now to call it moonshine?
His picture curls and yellows with the years
while verses, prompted from beyond, remain

for us to read and say by heart, restoring
his dead, shrewd, credulous voice to life.

QUESTIONS ABOUT ELIZABETH BISHOP'S CLAVICHORD

Curtly mentioned in memoirs, letters—how
can we reconstitute its image now?

Was it bedecked with marquetry,
grinning with choicest ivory,

in short, the classiest keyboard
on the Eastern seaboard?

Or was it modester, a mere
well-tempered clavier

whose charm centered alone
in a congenial tone?

(Mining another source just now, I'm told
the case's color scheme was green and gold.)

But further: what did an item like that fetch
when she ordered it from Dolmetsch?

When her nerves were taut and jangling,
did it subdue them with its twangling?

Past midnight, did she sway above its tune
while her Man-Moth flittered up, up toward the moon,

warding away malaise, alarm, fatigue
with a gavotte or gigue?

Did she ever play a prelude on it for
her mentor Marianne Moore,

or master her technique at last so well
as to regale Robert Lowell

with a Galuppian sonata
while he imbibed his vodka & Salada?

Did she play études dutifully until
fate whirled her off to sambas in Brazil?

Did she absorb a loss
when she sold it finally to Howard Moss?

(As losses go, this needn't have been bruising,
but did it help her learn the art of losing?)

What favored party did it pass to, when
HM in his turn went beyond our ken?

Just where might it reside now? In
the silence of a shadowy storage bin?

Or is it kept from such cobwebbed malingering
by some baroque fan's heavy fingering?

Distempered thus from hammering overmuch,
does it, like us, lament her lighter touch

too rare in any art this noisy while
since she departed with her pliant style,

leaving to blunter hands not only these
but her beloved ABC-clad keys,

each note there too struck silvery and sure,
so that her work, our wonder, both endure?

SINGLE FILE

It is your destiny to stand in line:
some, as it happens, are ahead of you.
However you may question the design,

this is the way it has to be. Don't whine.
Don't bother cursing that bad hand you drew.
It is your destiny to stand in line,

barred from all decent pretexts to resign.
You're here, you're late. While itching to squeeze through,
however, you may question the design:

Will it be worth the wait? That glass of wine?
That corner table with an ocean view?
It is your destiny. To stand in line

to have your passport stamped, your blood drawn, dine
deluxe or at some diner, this you do
however you may question. The design

is snarled in the future's ball of twine,
trailing an end you catch at for a clue.
It is your destiny to stand in line—
how? Ever. (You may question the design.)

OLD MAN OF THE MOUNTAIN

Charisma shaped his overhanging ledge,
made him iconic, heading him toward fame.
Eons on Cannon Mountain's windy edge
earned him his name.

After untold millennia, who counts?
That bare peak was his post. He stayed to man it,
staring at air and eagles, other mounts
made too of granite:

the constant sentinel who stole the scene.
His beetling brow, his massive lantern jaw,
his knife-edge nose protruding in between
indifferently cast awe

on the first scouts who pioneered the Notch,
tiptoeing past the shade of that profile.
Then followed tourist hordes to watch him watch,
with no hint of a smile,

the forests turn to farms, the straighter road
reform the ragged, snaking Indian trail.
None of these changes seemed much to forebode
a finis to his tale,

since none could change his vigil over change.
Then, one night, a vibration broke the spell.
Loosed from his lookout, leaving it vacant, strange,
his face fell.

Loss by a landslide made a sad enough
end to the reign of this New England sphinx;
sadder, to know his pose was one great bluff
riddled with chinks.

IN THE PICTURE

The M.D., as it says on his neat sign,
is neatly specialized. He treats The Hand.
Professionally caressing one of mine,
he doesn't hesitate to reach the point
in terms that even I can understand:
"You have arthritis in your left thumb joint."

He caught it on the X-ray. There it shows,
right where it shouldn't be, the site of pain
between two chalk-pegs, passing out the woes
just taking hold of things can leave me feeling.
What is it like? Annoying. Like a sprain
that re-emerges fresh from every healing.

For all of that, the pain's not often serious,
not halfway up his scale of one to ten,
I tell him, peering at the splayed, mysterious
image of my extremity fluoresced
against a field of darkness. (Now and then,
maybe, it hits a six.) Well, who'd have guessed

this would be where the first outbreak would come?
Never left-handed, I've demanded little
of this inflamed, opposable, sore thumb,
would even pay to have these flare-ups cease.
But any truce in such a spot is brittle.
Unfazed by film, aching to breach the peace,

this will persist. It could intensify,
exporting discontent to other zones.
The doctor of The Hand will have a try,
then hand me to a different specialist.
Meanwhile, in that precinct between bones,
resentment churns each time I make a fist.

WORKING OUT

Motivation

Mens sana in corpore sano might
be every bit as true as it is trite,
but what can spur the sedentary will
recurrently to gulp the bitter pill
of sane exertion? Doctor's orders. Fright.

*

Trainer

Hannah can see that I am too ethereal.
Her regimens are thoughtfully designed
to keep me focused on the raw material
that for so long had somehow slipped my mind.

*

Treadmill

A line from Hopkins trundles through my head:
"Generations have trod, have trod, have trod."
To keep alive I mime the trooping dead.
Ten minutes more must go to this sheer plod.

*

Rower

Charon, your moldy prow is faintly showing
on the horizon; in my dry-docked craft
I pull against an unseen current, knowing
there is no knowing just when you'll swing aft.

*

Pullups

My two arms dragging up the rest of me
are painfully apprised of gravity.

*

Situps

My brain says I should do five more now, but
a differing opinion fills my gut.

*

Bench Press

Peculiar, upward thrusting: like inverted
pushups, or attempting to get rid
of a blithe Saint Bernard. Or, disconcerted,
coaxing aloft a lowering coffin lid.

Attention-Getter

His clanking on of fifty extra pounds
is followed by a train of ardent sounds,
each beefy heave accompanied by grunts
which fail to charm us less ambitious runts.

*

Role Model

Past eighty-seven, at a queenly pace,
she gets her money's worth out of the place,
bestowing on each Nautilus machine,
to the mind's eye, an opalescent sheen.

*

Locker Room

So: am I still committed? All the more so;
what if each sinew creaks from recent strife?
A glance at this or that archaic torso
reminds me I had better change my life.

THRESHOLDS

The room was dark, too dark to see
ahead to what was wall or door.
Impeded with uncertainty,
he sought to reckon where the floor

might run (it helped to know his height).
And then he saw it, like a line
ruled low upon a blackboard: light.
A minimalist exit sign,

scant, but enough to make the scope
of his environs known to him.
Years later, when he looked for hope
to get him past a shadow's rim,

he thought of how the narrow gleam
restored dimension to the gloom,
and how like shrugging off a dream
it felt to leave that shuttered room.

HILL TOWNS IN WINTER

Then there is this portion of road that seems
a detour into the nineteenth century,
looping black and ribbony, swale at each side
packed below seasonal crust. First skirting slopes
studded with those ramshackle trunks that only
the wind bothers to fell, where snow can linger
sometimes well into spring, it veers to bisect
village centers that huddle sullen and cowed,
pistolwhipped by the weather, each stark white house
a block of ice presiding in a blank yard.
Only the shoveled footpaths reassure us
that such clumps of durance are inhabited,
since no one ever steps out to take the air
as we drive past all this en route to Pittsfield.

The life inside—is it old New England still,
hived but mildly humming in hibernation?
Soothing to imagine those households, guarded
each by a tapering frieze of icicles,
wise in the ways of waiting out the winter.
The quilt to piece, the loose chair-rung to reglue,
baked-apple-dessert smells, games of Parcheesi,
kittens chasing their tails to watch. And always
the twirl and slide of needles replicating
the pairs of mittens shedding mist by the stove.
Say it could be so, it remains beyond us.

The true pulse of each place stays boxed in clapboard,
busy with it knows what. It's wiser to mind
our own business, forgo time-travel, and keep
our eyes on the road. Just now, rounding a tight
curve, we've almost run into an ambulance,
halted silent behind a police car, both
flashing their frantic lights in garish contrast
to that drab colonial they have stopped at.
Though still no human figure enters the scene
in the combustive moment of our passing,
here's a reminder—by no means a relief—
that something, yes, is happening there inside,
while the gray uprush from the central chimney
(the last thing we can see as the road rises)
signals nothing, and signals it to no one.

PARABLE OF THE BIRDS

They might be swallows. Barely to be seen,
they comb through what the combine left behind,
dispersed, discreet, below the radar screen
while burnished stubble gives them grain to find;

till suddenly, as though at some behest
we cannot hear but they innately share,
they've catapulted up and coalesced
before we know it, mustered in midair

in so close-knit a flock it's more a swarm.
Swung in a cluster, seized by one intent,
they could enact how scattered inklings form
the mass and movement of an argument,

or even how a poet's hunt for words
might arouse images at ease in sky.
Too neat a likeness? Defter yet, the birds
will take their bearings, never going high,

and glide, unshackled from similitude,
down to the next field for newer gleaning.
The landscape they blend into, finding food,
is one the restless eye still raids for meaning.

ONE BLACK SQUIRREL

Skirmishing under the birdfeeder, these four
   gray squirrels are beginning to show
seasonal wear as they dredge through husk-piles for
   some actual seed. The latest snow

hasn't added grace to their dispositions;
   they snatch, butt, and scuffle to survive.
A palimpsest of tramplings, of collisions,
   forms under their scrum. It seems they thrive

first by bickering, then by minding the store—
   all in all, a glum crowd to survey . . .
which makes this sudden newcomer all the more
   a standout against the fretful, gray,

unchummy roughhousing of that sad quartet.
   His India-ink-steeped complexion
jolts the backbiters, leaving them "freaked with jet"
   (Milton, in another connection).

And for us, his foray's choreography,
   so sinuous we could almost clap,
makes its mark finally as calligraphy
   swirled across a broad sheet of foolscap,

all of his craft poured into each arabesque
   till his transporting runes have speeded
him to the treeline. Darting from this his desk,
   he brings to mind ours. Seen and heeded,

dashing it off so deftly and then dashing,
   he's dropped hints for one good way to write:
Firm pacing. Rapid pivots. No rehashing.
   Images made fast in black and white.

RIVER AND ROAD

Four days a week and sometimes five
I take my make-my-living drive
along a road I know too well.
For several miles, parallel
to mine, a river steers its course,
moving with unassuming force,
tugging its ripple-convoy south,
aiming to catch up with its mouth.
Till at a bridge we intersect
we each, in different ways, reflect:
I mull on all I need to do
while it absorbs the local view.
Absorbs? Well, no. Its surface proffers
back every sight each instant offers.
Leaves flutter from a lowdown limb
not only near but on the brim.
Glance up or down: the doubled sky
confounds a sense of low and high.
Each cloud flotilla setting sail
rates an escort in mirrored mail;
and, in the midst of all, the sun's
photons arouse rebounding ones.

If the road tended closer in
the water might display my twin,
but ferried on by asphalt, I'm
oblivious of it for the time.

Crossing from bank to bank, I go
my way and leave it to its flow.
What comes to pass upon its face
jars not a bit the river's pace.

And this goes on for days, for years.
As though through its own mist of tears
it gives the world back with a wink.
In me, though, such impressions sink
abeyant to a rambling grotto
(Room For It All might be its motto),
waiting spellbound or simply parked
for days or decades unremarked
till, surging from the silt to break
the placid surface with their wake,
they win the notice I'd withheld
before. I let our currents meld,
returning buoyancy and sheen
to a long-disregarded scene
now entertained in full and made
part of my conscious cavalcade—
with such a feeling, maybe, as
the steady-running river has
when it arrives to meet the sea
and finds a mightier harmony.
And, so it won't drop out of sight
once more, I take my pen and write.

A BEGINNING, A MIDDLE, AND AN END

I

This happens sometimes: tumbling down a stream
after a storm, a rack of driftwood snags
on a rocklip just barely underwater,
and stays there long enough to start a small
amalgamation of like-ferried flotsam,
fashioning something like a beaver dam.
Silt collects, clotting the soggy matrix
eddy by eddy, particle after particle,
until in a dry summer you can see
a muddy knob making itself known,
ringed green by waterweed and finally
(this can take years) sporting a coarse cap
of grass seeded by wind and lisping currents.
Ecce: an island. All it took was time,
a lot of racing water and lazy dirt,
and the habitual inattentiveness
that led you to forget it every time
it met your eye, allowing it to grow
season by season into something you
at last find too substantial to ignore.
It had its own beginnings, but you missed them.
You weren't keyed in to the confluence.
For you, then, the beginning is the day
the place appears fit to welcome drifters

of a more sentient type. Ready to venture,
you feel the word *alluvial* on your tongue,
nestled like a bland gelatinous slab.

II

Splashing the two or three steps across, you take
possession of the spot, first colonist.
A few square feet: not much here to explore
or to exploit, except for your impression
of standing in the middle of a world.
Little to look at means you start to listen.
You notice how the sound the ripples make
upstream is different from the downstream sound—
a faint, pebbly variance in pitch.
You muse over the stereo effect
idling on your tussock, watching water
bustling right and left along its channels,
sparkling from the sun straight overhead.
All very Heraclitean and, if one
were candid, something of an anticlimax.
You wonder why you bothered. Sun pelts down.
Birds are cloistered, silent. Dragonflies
dart after midges, glinting neon blue.
Fixed in the middle, what is here for you?

III

Obviously you need a second character.
Wait long enough and nature will oblige.
Some yards away on the opposite bank, a patch
of woods draws your attention. At the treeline,
the weeds and brambles part without a sound
and out into the floodlit grass a fox
paces with the accustomed bored aplomb
of one who's never, ever missed a cue.
His dusty red coat could use some grooming;
his scrawny flanks are starred with beggar's lice.
He might be thirsty—it is a hot, still day.
He notices you instantly, although
you haven't let go the least noise or motion.
Looking at you installed like some ungainly
colossus at the center of his stream,
his yellow eyes transmit a message so
easy to read it's almost audible:
Man, what are you after?
                    After a moment,
caution preempts his peevish curiosity
and, with an ostentatious lack of hurry,
he turns and walks away, re-entering
the undergrowth without a backward look,
but with a last impatient flick of tail.

Perhaps the poem could end here, as indeed
more than a few notable poems have done;
but for you, how conclusive is his exit?
Self-marooned midstream, you still are learning
how much of life consists of coda. Maybe
someday you will ford that second moat
(even though you know he wasn't beckoning)
and leave behind that farther bank to follow
his auburn flourish into the green shade,
and find an end—unless by then you've found
that what you're after is a new beginning.

IN STORAGE: A CALDER CAT

Curious interlopers in our households,
they come and go. And when they go for good
the ones that oddly deigned to live with us
enter a tenth life of family legend,
or say of leitmotif, always beginning
"That was the one." That was the one who caught
a bat on the roof and brought it in the window.
That was the one who always swallowed string.
That was the one who died, sadly enough,
when a tinned ham slid off the kitchen counter.
Note how often the theme is appetite.
But this one? There's no tidbit to entice him.
Between svelte and scrawny, like some we've known,
able to appear both round and flat,
lolling with one nonchalant front paw
crossed on the other, but with ears a-cock,
the negligible peg of a tail perked up
assertively—as anyone can see,
his nose is out of joint. One is not moved
to pet that coat of what looks like scuffed umber
shoe polish rubbed over streaks and whorls
of wood graining that here stand in for stripes.
But see the eyes of this barn-timber idol.
Idol or Eye Doll? Bulging like a pair
of tethered blimps, those eyes return our stare,
triggering us to blink first, intimating

that *we* are the truant pupils come to take
instruction or correction in this sanctum
of storage cabinets, the inmost shrine.
Fresh from this pilgrimage, I'd recommend
this cat stay in the cupboard. He's not one
we can imagine willing to adopt us.
Homely, heraldic, too sedate to spit,
this wooden totem's scorn for us is total.
This is the one we wince to think of, watching
even after the metal door swings shut.

CAT'S AFTERNOON

It's tiring keeping up your killing skills
where mice are non-existent. String is string,
all right to wrestle with in daily drills,
but finally not the most exciting thing.

All his alertness needs to have a break,
and washing those already spotless paws
is more than he desires to undertake
just now. A great yawn opens wide his jaws,

and when he finds a sun pool on the floor,
he doesn't hesitate to take the plunge.
He stretches out full-length, then stretches more,
or so it seems, an ardent furry sponge

soaking up photons. Through the closing gap
between his leisured eyelids he can see
no earthly reason not to take a nap.
Sidling past, we're tempted to agree,

except that errands call us, and we lack
that settled mien that makes the world a spa.
He'll want his supper by the time we're back.
For now, he'll doze and worship Amun-Ra.

A REAPPEARANCE

Our childhood epic car trip took us
through wide, flat states whose vistas maintained
sameness for most of the two long days.
We gave up counting the truck-tire treads
that littered the apron like the cast
skins of anacondas, and likewise
we gave up on cows, though we were told
they were a sight for suburban eyes.
More corn than cows whipped by anyway,
packed and rocketing tall and tasseled,
punctuated by tin-capped silos,
big brothers to the sugar shakers
in the roadside diners we stopped at.
They were not too exciting, either.
Even the odd quixotic windmill
that we might glimpse occasionally,
malingering in the windless heat,
came to appear monotony's pawn.
Before us by a few hundred yards,
always keeping that distance from us,
there was one thing that claimed attention
without turning stale through afternoon's
hours of hard glare: spilling across
the highway in a dark, narrow band
what looked like a shallow, pulsing stream.
Being informed it was a mirage

didn't defuse its tantalizing
hint of some prize the road's hypnotic
straight-as-a-die trajectory might
at last succeed in bringing us to.

I haven't seen it too often since,
the roads I drive being rarely straight
and often shadowed, but yesterday,
on a straight stretch, there it was again,
just as wet-looking, carrying out
its placid charade. I tried to fish
a memory up of how I used
to imagine it might feel and taste
if we could ever catch up with it.
Wonderfully cold, I had decided,
back there and then; but here and now, I
wonder if it hasn't grown tepid,
bored with purveying summer pipe dreams
to children bound to see through them soon.

WARM SPELL IN MARCH

The thinning coverage of the snow
has left an archipelago—
white islands dwindling in between
crosscurrents of encroaching green.
Overhead, clouds ape the effect,
except the ocean they elect
to linger in's a different hue.
Below, above us, green and blue,
spring tides are coming in, and we
can feel a wave of buoyancy
chopping at winter's crumbling shore.
Imagine us, marooned no more,
rafting to warmer latitudes,
and longer days, and lighter moods.
It ought to be the simplest thing
to greet the flooding in of spring,
but still, a wisp of worry forms.
We've grown too used to weekly storms,
and now must strain to make the shift
from Being Pent to Set Adrift,
wondering when adversity
might burst from this uncharted sea.
Not that we'll miss our melting isle,
but confidence may take a while.

AN ETYMOLOGY

It used to captivate me as a child:
tipping the pitcher gingerly to the glass,
I'd fill it up till it was more than filled,
the water mounding up above the brim
in a dome, low but evident in profile,
that melded substance with transparency.
A hummock of unruffled concentration,
taut but not tense, the nub of H_2O
stood undisturbed until it was disturbed—
by what, I never knew. A breath, a nudge
from its surroundings broke its magic poise,
slashed invisible cords of surface tension,
and fountained water down, the outer wall
becoming just as wet as that inside.
Some Bible lessons made me think of it:
things like the angel troubling the waters,
or "my cup runneth over." Later on,
I found a name for that ephemeral
amassing in my glass: the word *meniscus*,
which means in Greek a little (crescent) moon,
and also means a type of convex lens.
And that made sense to me. I could recall
the way the trim, cylindrically boosted
bulge of water like a cyclops eye
seemed to be taking in all within range
until whatever happened to it happened,

dissolving it to a quick flow of tears.
And what about the moon? The crescent wanes,
but waxes too. The glass can be refilled.

THIRST AT MIDNIGHT

Looking through the skylight
a moment after midnight,
I found my gaze returned.
The seven bright eyes burned
with neither love nor hate.
Aloof, they constellate
in what we choose to call
the Dipper (Big, not small).
It seemed in line with why
I'd gotten up—mouth dry—
but I would get no sips
from its galactic dips.
We know now that the stars
can't succor human scars,
can't (in this case) fill up
a single bathroom cup.
We know, we know, we know.
Why did I linger so,
in search of something there
behind the white-hot stare?
Did I expect a drop
of nectar from up top
to trickle down and spike, or
transmute my blood to ichor?
How many kinds of thirst
had I in darkness nursed?

Scuffing a loose slipper,
I stared back at the Dipper—
too long. Then gripped the sink,
and got myself a drink.

DONORS

(Altarpiece of the Annunciation,
by Robert Campin of Tournai, c. 1425)

In this dull town it's just another workday,
at least for those who work. The carpenter,
off to the right in his side-panel shop,
grizzled and loosely turbaned, plies his tools,
adding finishing touches to a mousetrap,
aiming to match one on his windowsill.
If only he'd invent a better model
the world, they say, would beat a path to his door;
but as it is, no customers intrude
upon his placid bouts of joinery.

In the next, nicer room his so-much-younger
bride nestles against a settlebench,
chores of the morning done. She is profoundly
lost in the book she's reading, which her careful
housekeeping has dust-proofed in white linen.
Wrapped in a crimson robe whose crumpled damask
folds and peaks return a light not earthly,
she has not yet glanced up to see the winged
informant who with her shares center stage;
and he seems bashful, diffident to break
the spell her eyes are held by. On the table
a candle just extinguished lets a tuft
of smoke escape—the wick put out, perhaps,
by the guest's entering flutter. Everything

is tidy otherwise; the polished brass
of the washpot, the fresh towel on the rack,
the lilies in the jug will not for long
divert us from the prodigy now bound
to infiltrate their order. Through the diamond-
leading of the glass behind the angel
a naked, ghostly-white homunculus
no bigger than a hummingbird glides down,
cleaving air on a sheaf of golden beams,
carrying his cross like a child's plaything
toward a beginning and its certain end.

And all the while that this is going on,
sequestered in a panel at the left,
the donors, Mr. and Mrs. Inglebrecht,
kneel in the courtyard, gazing ill-at-ease
through the swung-open door at Mystery
making itself at home. Dark-clad, a bit
on edge for all their *bürgerlich* deportment,
they could be neighbors who have stepped across
to borrow salt or venture a complaint,
or landlords dropping by to take the rent.
A pity they should feel so out of place
when their own coat-of-arms emblazoned glows
from a high windowpane. But there it is:

no matter what their errand they must wait
cooling their heels and punishing their knees
between the rosebush and the clean doorstep
while curiosity consorts with fear.
They watch as miracle prepares to happen,
making them after all like us in giving
all their attention to the central scene,
giving their mundane selves up to this moment
before the angel speaks to end the silence
with the incredible ordaining words.

RATTLES

I

A man whose mother
threw nothing out
sorts through relics
of infancy:
a bib, a teether,
and a blue plastic
rattle that sounds
like a peppercorn jar
picked up and jiggled.
Scaled to a highchair
percussionist's fist,
shaped like a cartoon
dumbbell, this
enabled his first
performances, letting
expression loose:
not saying *Here
I am* (for that
he just had to yell),
but sharing a boast:
*The noise I make
each time I shake
is something I've learned
to do and do well.*

II

In rocky places
the diamondback
adds to its rack
of resonators
each time it drops
an outgrown skin.
Flicking its tail
transmits that famous
warning (a noise
outdoing the rasp
of irate cicadas):
Keep your distance.
I've got a dose
of death-rattle ready
for absentminded
owners of ankles
that come too close.

III

Something akin
but yet so different
dances in memory—
dry but lively
seeds in a gourd,
shaken to help
the seasons happen,
send up word
from the canyon floor:
Come all together,
remind the sun
how fine a circle
we make down here,
held by the sound
of the harvest rattle
leading our steps
on dusty ground.

A CERTAIN OTHER SLANT

It's funny the way we say it's time to unbend
when we mean bend: dismiss the parade-ground posture,
lean with the way of the world this easy morning.
See the blinds partly askew, parsing the sun-flood
into a radiant sheaf of diagonals,
combing the bedroom rug with rich obliquity.
Where would we be without the earth's reliable
tilt that summons up summer? We should welcome it,
remembering all the gentle green gradations
leading here and beyond that give the long shadow
of the most upright tree a hammock to sag on.

Beautiful the pitch of our roof, lightly steaming
as dew takes its leave by a throng of unmapped paths.
Beautiful the moist grass, pliant beneath each breeze.
Beautiful the slope of the horse's tousled neck
as he champs his own grass in the field down the road.
But why go even that far to scout out angles?
Beautiful, just now, your inclination toward me.

SUNDIAL IN THE RAIN

Patiently waiting for the sun to rise,
the dial seems more dutiful than wise:
the sun, already up for hours, seems
a shrouded moon, so muted are its beams.
Mist complicates to drizzle, then to drops.
Like one of Thomas Hardy's dismal props,
demure atop its neo-Gothic column,
the timepiece tenders us that old, unsolemn
advisory: it counts only sunny hours.
If one subtracts for night, for clouds, for showers,
that hardly makes a taxing regimen.
Always willing to work, of course, but when
is not for it or us to specify,
much as we might prefer to clear the sky.

The gnomon, less a pointer than a nose
of stiff wrought iron, juts aloft and shows
there isn't anything to do but wait,
unless to smell dank earth and meditate
on times we're just as willing not to mark.
Could we surrender to the larger dark
the shadows that our memories renew,
it would be no great trick to share the view
that keeps the dial jovially on track.
It never forfeits time in looking back,
endures inertia while the meddling storm

denies it freedom to project its form,
and holding its potential in good stead
resumes its reach as quick as light is shed.

BLUE PERIOD SKETCH

Stepping outside for once without my key,
I heard the latch click like fatality.
I felt my pockets, called myself a name
(there being no one else around to blame),
tried other doors (although I knew them locked,
leaving me self-excluded, self-bemocked).
I felt like someone's dog or cat, whose only
way to get in is to sit looking lonely
until the door mysteriously swings wide
enough to let him hustle back inside.
I pulled some weeds, then settled on a bench,
waiting to feel my wound-up nerves unclench,
and having given vent to irritation,
warily lent myself to rustication.

Well, as we all know, nothing happens when
we're on the lookout for it. Nothing then
occurred that I could not have seen if I
had chosen any day to play the spy,
guarding the garden like a sentient gnome,
familiarly displaced, strangely at home.
A pair of crows, disputing territory,
shouted out insults, grim and minatory.
A meditative cloud dispensing shade
at the yard's far end curbed its promenade
and hung at rest in a breath-catching hover.

The neighbor's cat, disgruntled to discover
a witness to his trespass, crossed the lawn,
oozed through a row of cypress and was gone.
I looked back at the sky. The cloud had drifted
after all, while my gaze had dropped and shifted.
And there it was: the sky my childhood knew.
Unbounded, elevated depths of blue
into which, lying flat on grass, I'd stare
and find no end to openness up there—
so deep a reach of blue I thought the sky's
immensity might overfill my eyes,
adding its essence to their film of tears.
I hadn't seen it quite that way for years.

For an arrested moment, though, I did.
And if the eye by lowering its lid
could hold a sight forever, I would still
be hypnotized, surveying heaven's sill.
I would be still upheld in strange rapport
with cloudless calm last met so long before.
Its vibrancy was something elemental
(or, this being New England, transcendental).

I lost it, though, the instant that I blinked.
My grasp of it grew somehow less distinct;
the present slid uncoupled from the past;

the moment, like all moments, couldn't last.
However close we'd seemed to interfusion,
the sky and I, it was the same illusion
I had let go of, or been let go by,
once days were gone when I had time for sky.
The blue withdrew itself, intact, unfading,
even as I felt drained of its pervading.
What had I wanted it to do? Imbue me,
spreading its otherworldly tint all through me?
(*Beneath* the skin—if topically bestowed,
I'd stand out, like a druid daubed with woad.)
A chasm that had narrowed to a crack
had yawned again. My separateness was back.
Communion decomposing, I was left
with one more way in which to feel bereft;
so I was more than ready when my wife
restored me to the round of daily life
by coming home and lending me her key,
while trying not to laugh too much at me.

DUSK

Although the child knew the grown-up word
was not the same as *dust*, as dark invaded,
she thought of something dust-like when she heard
the old poetic term. When daylight faded,

what she believed appeared there was a host
of milling motes intent to occupy,
from ground to zenith and from coast to coast,
the ambient air and all the loftier sky—

each monad too diminutive to see
singly, of course, but in the aggregate
composing darkness as it grew to be
the ruling power after sun had set.

Not a particularly (or partic-
ulately) pleasant way for night to form.
Fortunately, the vision didn't stick.
As years went by, she blinked away the swarm.

She pays less notice now when evening falls.
Dawn is what draws her; someday she may trust
its pantomime of what an old prayer calls
the radiance that lies behind our dust.

OUT FOR SOME AIR

That sofa looks like one we used to have.
Whatever happened to it, ours was not
disposed of quite so publicly as this one,
sitting close to the curb on this warm day
in early May, the apex of spring cleaning.

It's had a life—that, no one could deny.
Its back and arms are pocked with random snags,
the work of cats testing their weaponry;
and there's a fading of its floral print
from years of daily raking by the sun.
Near to one end a brownish sort of stain
was no doubt classified as a disaster
before devolving into something less—
a blotch that could be lived with. For a time.
Subduing their own censure, people sat
considering slipcovers as a stopgap
and thinking: After all, the springs are good.
(As they are even now—the heavy uncles,
semi-sedated by weekend TV,
failed to saddle it with a lasting sag.)

But the indulgence, thrift, or lassitude
that kept it on the job is at an end.
Suddenly its horizons have expanded,
and it appears unnervingly upbeat,

ready for some unprecedented turn
of fortune (if a sofa can be said
to be subject to fortune, good or bad).
Trying it as a perch, a chickadee
swivels his head, surveys us quizzically,
then leaves like someone vacating a park bench.
This was supposed to be a walk, but now
we're almost tempted to sit down on this
upholstered refugee from thoughtless use
and contemplate the future, its and ours,
on this, an ideal day to be outdoors.

CPSIA information can be obtained at www.ICGtesting.com
Printed in the USA
268196BV00002B/38/P